12/01/18

D0835460

SR

POETRY PLEASE
The Seasons

POETRY PLEASE

The Seasons

FABER & FABER

First published in 2015
by Faber & Faber Ltd
Bloomsbury House
74–77 Great Russell Street
London WC1B 3DA

Typeset by RefineCatch Ltd, Bungay, Suffolk
Printed and bound in England by
CPI Group (UK) Ltd, Croydon, CRO 4YY

A CIP record for this book
is available from the British Library

ISBN 978-0-571-32545-0

2 4 6 8 10 9 7 5 3 1

Contents

❧

SPRING

~

POETRY PLEASE

The Seasons

The Human Seasons

Four Seasons fill the measure of the year;
   There are four seasons in the mind of man:
He has his lusty Spring, when fancy clear
   Takes in all beauty with an easy span:
He has his Summer, when luxuriously
   Spring's honied cud of youthful thought he loves
To ruminate, and by such dreaming high
   Is nearest unto heaven: quiet coves
His soul has in its Autumn, when his wings
   He furleth close; contented so to look
On mists in idleness – to let fair things
   Pass by unheeded as a threshold brook.
He has his Winter too of pale misfeature,
Or else he would forego his mortal nature.

JOHN KEATS

A Song for England

An' a so de rain a-fall
An' a so de snow a-rain

An' a so de fog a-fall
An' a so de sun a-fail

An' a so de seasons mix
An' a so de bag-o-tricks

But a so me understan'
De misery o' de Englishman.

ANDREW SALKEY

The Twelve Months

Snowy, Flowy, Blowy,
Showery, Flowery, Bowery,
Hoppy, Croppy, Droppy,
Breezy, Sneezy, Freezy.

GEORGE ELLIS

WINTER

Birds at Winter Nightfall

Around the house the flakes fly faster,
And all the berries now are gone
From holly and cotoneaster
Around the house. The flakes fly! faster
Shutting indoors that crumb-outcaster
We used to see upon the lawn
Around the house. The flakes fly faster,
And all the berries now are gone!

THOMAS HARDY

Ceremonies for Candlemasse Eve

Down with the Rosemary and Bayes,
　　　Down with the Mistleto;
In stead of Holly, now up-raise
　　　The greener Box (for show).

The Holly hitherto did sway;
　　　Let Box now domineere;
Untill the dancing Easter-day,
　　　Or Easters Eve appeare.

Then youthfull Box which now hath grace,
　　　Your houses to renew;
Grown old, surrender must his place,
　　　Unto the crisped Yew.

When Yew is out, then Birch comes in,
　　　And many Flowers beside;
Both of a fresh, and fragrant kinne
　　　To honour Whitsontide.

Green Rushes then, and sweetest Bents,
　　　With cooler Oken boughs;
Come in for comely ornaments,
　　　To re-adorn the house.
Thus times do shift; each thing his turne do's hold;
New things succeed, as former things grow old.

ROBERT HERRICK

A Christmas Carol

In the bleak mid-winter
    Frosty wind made moan,
Earth stood hard as iron,
    Water like a stone;
Snow had fallen, snow on snow,
    Snow on snow,
In the bleak mid-winter
    Long ago.

Our God, Heaven cannot hold Him
    Nor earth sustain;
Heaven and earth shall flee away
    When He comes to reign:
In the bleak mid-winter
    A stable-place sufficed
The Lord God Almighty
    Jesus Christ.

Enough for Him whom cherubim
    Worship night and day,
A breastful of milk
    And a mangerful of hay;
Enough for Him whom angels
    Fall down before,
The ox and ass and camel
    Which adore.

Angels and archangels
    May have gathered there,
Cherubim and seraphim
    Throng'd the air,
But only His mother
    In her maiden bliss
Worshipped the Beloved
    With a kiss.

What can I give Him,
    Poor as I am?
If I were a shepherd
    I would bring a lamb,
If I were a wise man
    I would do my part, –
Yet what I can I give Him,
    Give my heart.

CHRISTINA ROSSETTI

The Christmas Life

*'If you don't have a real tree, you don't bring the
Christmas life into the house.'*
– JOSEPHINE MACKINNON, AGED 8

Bring in a tree, a young Norwegian spruce,
Bring hyacinths that rooted in the cold.
Bring winter jasmine as its buds unfold –
Bring the Christmas life into this house.

Bring red and green and gold, bring things that shine,
Bring candlesticks and music, food and wine.
Bring in your memories of Christmas past.
Bring in your tears for all that you have lost.

Bring in the shepherd boy, the ox and ass,
Bring in the stillness of an icy night,
Bring in a birth, of hope and love and light.
Bring the Christmas life into this house.

WENDY COPE

Frost at Midnight

The frost performs its secret ministry,
Unhelped by any wind. The owlet's cry
Came loud – and hark, again! loud as before.
The inmates of my cottage, all at rest,
Have left me to that solitude, which suits
Abstruser musings: save that at my side
My cradled infant slumbers peacefully.
'Tis calm indeed! so calm, that it disturbs
And vexes meditation with its strange
And extreme silentness. Sea, hill, and wood,
This populous village! Sea, and hill, and wood,
With all the numberless goings on of life,
Inaudible as dreams! the thin blue flame
Lies on my low burnt fire, and quivers not;
Only that film, which fluttered on the grate,
Still flutters there, the sole unquiet thing.
Methinks, its motion in this hush of nature
Gives it dim sympathies with me who live,
Making it a companionable form,
Whose puny flaps and freaks the idling Spirit
By its own moods interprets, every where
Echo or mirror seeking of itself,
And makes a toy of Thought.

                                    But O! how oft,
How oft, at school, with most believing mind,
Presageful, have I gazed upon the bars,
To watch that fluttering stranger! and as oft
With unclosed lids, already had I dreamt
Of my sweet birth-place, and the old church tower

Whose bells, the poor man's only music, rang
From morn to evening, all the hot Fair-day,
So sweetly, that they stirred and haunted me
With a wild pleasure, falling on mine ear
Most like articulate sounds of things to come!
So gazed I, till the soothing things I dreamt
Lulled me to sleep, and sleep prolonged my dreams!
And so I brooded all the following morn,
Awed by the stern preceptor's face, mine eye
Fixed with mock study on my swimming book:
Save if the door half opened, and I snatched
A hasty glance, and still my heart leaped up.
For still I hoped to see the stranger's face,
Townsman, or aunt, or sister more beloved,
My play-mate when we both were clothed alike!

  Dear Babe, that sleepest cradled by my side,
Whose gentle breathings, heard in this deep calm,
Fill up the interspersed vacancies
And momentary pauses of the thought!
My babe so beautiful! it thrills my heart
With tender gladness, thus to look at thee,
And think that thou shalt learn far other lore
And in far other scenes! For I was reared
In the great city, pent 'mid cloisters dim,
And saw nought lovely but the sky and stars.
But thou, my babe! shalt wander like a breeze
By lakes and sandy shores, beneath the crags
Of ancient mountain, and beneath the clouds,
Which image in their bulk both lakes and shores
And mountain crags: so shalt thou see and hear
The lovely shapes and sounds intelligible
Of that eternal language, which thy God

Utters, who from eternity doth teach
Himself in all, and all things in himself.
Great universal Teacher! he shall mould
Thy spirit, and by giving make it ask.

Therefore all seasons shall be sweet to thee,
Whether the summer clothe the general earth
With greenness, or the redbreast sit and sing
Betwixt the tufts of snow on the bare branch
Of mossy apple-tree, while the nigh thatch
Smokes in the sun-thaw; whether the eave-drops fall
Heard only in the trances of the blast,
Or if the secret ministry of frost
Shall hang them up in silent icicles,
Quietly shining to the quiet Moon.

SAMUEL TAYLOR COLERIDGE

A Frosty Day

Grass afield wears silver thatch;
   Palings all are edged with rime;
Frost-flowers pattern round the latch;
   Cloud nor breeze dissolve the clime;

When the waves are solid floor,
   And the clods are iron-bound,
And the boughs are crystall'd hoar,
   And the red leaf nailed a-ground.

When the fieldfare's flight is slow,
   And a rosy vapour rim,
Now the sun is small and low,
   Belts along the region dim.

When the ice-crack flies and flaws,
   Shore to shore, with thunder shock,
Deeper than the evening daws,
   Clearer than the village clock.

When the rusty blackbird strips,
   Bunch by bunch, the coral thorn;
And the pale day-crescent dips,
   Now to heaven, a slender horn.

LORD DE TABLEY

'The holly and the ivy'

The holly and the ivy,
When they are both full grown,
Of all the trees that are in the wood,
The holly bears the crown:

The rising of the sun
And the running of the deer,
The playing of the merry organ,
Sweet singing in the choir.

The holly bears a blossom,
As white as the lily flower,
And Mary bore sweet Jesus Christ,
To be our sweet Saviour:

The holly bears a berry,
As red as any blood,
And Mary bore sweet Jesus Christ
To do poor sinners good:

The holly bears a prickle,
As sharp as any thorn,
And Mary bore sweet Jesus Christ
On Christmas day in the morn:

TRAD.

Ice on the Highway

Seven buxom women abreast, and arm in arm,
  Trudge down the hill, tip-toed,
    And breathing warm;
They must perforce trudge thus, to keep upright
  On the glassy ice-bound road.

And they must get to market whether or no,
  Provisions running low
  With the nearing Saturday night,
While the lumbering van wherein they mostly ride
  Can nowise go:
Yet loud their laughter as they stagger and slide!

THOMAS HARDY

London Snow

When men were all asleep the snow came flying,
In large white flakes falling on the city brown,
Stealthily and perpetually settling and loosely lying,
   Hushing the latest traffic of the drowsy town;
Deadening, muffling, stifling its murmurs failing;
Lazily and incessantly floating down and down:
   Silently sifting and veiling road, roof and railing;
Hiding difference, making unevenness even,
Into angles and crevices softly drifting and sailing.
   All night it fell, and when full inches seven
It lay in the depth of its uncompacted lightness,
The clouds blew off from a high and frosty heaven;
   And all woke earlier for the unaccustomed brightness
Of the winter dawning, the strange unheavenly glare:
The eye marvelled – marvelled at the dazzling whiteness;
   The ear hearkened to the stillness of the solemn air;
No sound of wheel rumbling nor of foot falling,
And the busy morning cries came thin and spare.
   Then boys I heard, as they went to school, calling,
They gathered up the crystal manna to freeze
Their tongues with tasting, their hands with snowballing;
   Or rioted in a drift, plunging up to the knees;
Or peering up from under the white-mossed wonder,
'O look at the trees!' they cried, 'O look at the trees!'
   With lessened load a few carts creak and blunder,
Following along the white deserted way,
A country company long dispersed asunder:
   When now already the sun, in pale display
Standing by Paul's high dome, spread forth below
His sparkling beams, and awoke the stir of the day.

For now doors open, and war is waged with the snow;
And trains of sombre men, past tale of number,
Tread long brown paths, as toward their toil they go:
    But even for them awhile no cares encumber
Their minds diverted; the daily word is unspoken,
The daily thoughts of labour and sorrow slumber
At the sight of the beauty that greets them, for the charm
    they have broken.

ROBERT BRIDGES

Midwinter

Entranced, you turn again and over there
It is white also. Rectangular white lawns
For miles, white walls between them. Snow.
You close your eyes. The terrible changes.

White movements in one corner of your room.
Between your hands, the flowers of your quilt
Are stormed. Dark shadows smudge
Their faded, impossible colours, but won't settle.

You can hear the ice take hold.
Along the street
The yellowed drifts, cleansed by a minute's fall,
Wait to be fouled again. Your final breath
Is in the air, pure white, and moving fast.

IAN HAMILTON

'Now, Shepherds, to your helpless Charge be kind'

from Winter

Now, Shepherds, to your helpless Charge be kind,
Baffle the raging Year, and fill their Pens
With Food at Will; lodge them below the Storm,
And watch them strict: for from the bellowing East,
In this dire Season, oft the Whirlwind's Wing
Sweeps up the Burthen of whole wintry Plains
In one wide Waft, and o'er the hapless Flocks,
Hid in the Hollow of two neighbouring Hills,
The billowy Tempest whelms; till, upward urg'd,
The Valley to a shining Mountain swells,
Tipt with a Wreath, high-curling in the Sky.

As thus the Snows arise; and foul, and fierce,
All Winter drives along the darken'd Air;
In his own loose-revolving Fields, the Swain
Disaster'd stands; sees other Hills ascend,
Of unknown joyless Brow; and other Scenes,
Of horrid Prospect, shag the trackless Plain:
Nor finds the River, nor the Forest, hid
Beneath the formless Wild; but wanders on
From Hill to Dale, still more and more astray;
Impatient flouncing thro the drifted Heaps,
Stung with the Thoughts of Home; the Thoughts of Home
Rush on his Nerves, and call their Vigour forth
In many a vain Attempt. How sinks his Soul!
What black Despair, what Horror fills his Heart!
When for the dusky Spot, which Fancy feign'd
His tufted Cottage rising thro the Snow,

He meets the Roughness of the middle Waste,
Far from the Track, and blest Abode of Man;
While round him Night resistless closes fast,
And every Tempest, howling o'er his Head,
Renders the savage Wilderness more wild.
Then throng the busy Shapes into his Mind,
Of cover'd Pits, unfathomably deep,
A dire Descent! beyond the Power of Frost,
Of faithless Bogs; of Precipices huge,
Smooth'd up with Snow; and, what is Land unknown,
What Water, of the still unfrozen Spring,
In the loose Marsh or solitary Lake,
Where the fresh Fountain from the Bottom boils.
These check his fearful Steps; and down he sinks
Beneath the Shelter of the shapeless Drift,
Thinking o'er all the Bitterness of Death,
Mix'd with the tender Anguish Nature shoots
Thro the wrung Bosom of the dying Man,
His Wife, his Children, and his Friends unseen.
In vain for him th' officious Wife prepares
The Fire fair-blazing, and the Vestment warm;
In vain his little Children, peeping out
Into the mingling Storm, demand their Sire,
With Tears of artless Innocence. Alas!
Nor Wife, nor Children, more shall he behold,
Nor Friends, nor sacred Home. On every Nerve
The deadly Winter seizes; shuts up Sense;
And, o'er his inmost Vitals creeping cold,
Lays him along the Snows, a stiffen'd Corse,
Stretch'd out, and bleaching in the northern Blast.

JAMES THOMSON

'Now winter nights enlarge'

Now winter nights enlarge
The number of their hours,
And clouds their storms discharge
Upon the airy towers.
Let now the chimneys blaze,
And cups o'erflow with wine;
Let well-tuned words amaze
With harmony divine.
Now yellow waxen lights
Shall wait on honey love,
While youthful revels, masques, and courtly sights
Sleep's leaden spells remove.

This time doth well dispense
With lovers' long discourse;
Much speech hath some defence,
Though beauty no remorse.
All do not all things well;
Some measures comely tread,
Some knotted riddles tell,
Some poems smoothly read.
The summer hath his joys
And winter his delights;
Though love and all his pleasures are but toys,
They shorten tedious nights.

THOMAS CAMPION

Perfect Day

I am just a woman of the shore
wearing your coat against the snow
that falls on the oyster-catcher's tracks
and on our own; falls
on the still grey waters
of Loch Morar, and on our shoulders
gentle as restraint: a perfect weight
of snow as tree-boughs
and fences bear against a loaded sky:
one flake more, they'd break.

KATHLEEN JAMIE

Pieces of Unprofitable Land

The pieces of unprofitable land
are what I like, best seen in winter,
triangular tail of cottage garden
tall with dead willowherb, and tangled splinter
of uncut copse edging the red-ploughed fields,
and between hedge and headland of such fields
the slope of one-in-four the plough can't touch,
mayweed and old larks' nests its only yields.
In countryside so arable and fenced
that verges are the only common land
these roughs are memories of former wilds
untouched by foot, unharvested by hand.
Attained by sight alone, because so small,
private, or thorny, stuffed with the years' seeds,
their failure's proof of reclamation,
their vigour justifies all wastes and weeds.

MOLLY HOLDEN

A Robin

Ghost-grey the fall of night,
  Ice-bound the lane,
Lone in the dying light
  Flits he again;
Lurking where shadows steal,
Perched in his coat of blood,
Man's homestead at his heel,
  Death-still the wood.

Odd restless child; it's dark;
  All wings are flown
But this one wizard's – hark!
  Stone clapped on stone!
Changeling and solitary,
Secret and sharp and small,
Flits he from tree to tree,
  Calling on all.

WALTER DE LA MARE

Scotland's Winter

Now the ice lays its smooth claws on the sill,
The sun looks from the hill
Helmed in his winter casket,
And sweeps his arctic sword across the sky.
The water at the mill
Sounds more hoarse and dull.
The miller's daughter walking by
With frozen fingers soldered to her basket
Seems to be knocking
Upon a hundred leagues of floor
With her light heels, and mocking
Percy and Douglas dead,
And Bruce on his burial bed,
Where he lies white as may
With wars and leprosy,
And all the kings before
This land was kingless,
And all the singers before
This land was songless,
This land that with its dead and living waits the Judgement Day.
But they, the powerless dead,
Listening can hear no more
Than a hard tapping on the sounding floor
A little overhead
Of common heels that do not know
Whence they come or where they go
And are content
With their poor frozen life and shallow banishment.

EDWIN MUIR

Snow

The room was suddenly rich and the great bay-window
    was
Spawning snow and pink roses against it
Soundlessly collateral and incompatible:
World is suddener than we fancy it.

World is crazier and more of it than we think,
Incorrigibly plural. I peel and portion
A tangerine and spit the pips and feel
The drunkenness of things being various.

And the fire flames with a bubbling sound for world
Is more spiteful and gay than one supposes –
On the tongue on the eyes on the ears in the palms of one's
    hands –
There is more than glass between the snow and the huge
    roses.

LOUIS MACNEICE

Snow Storm

What a night! The wind howls, hisses, and but stops
To howl more loud, while the snow volley keeps
Incessant batter at the window pane,
Making our comfort feel as sweet again;
And in the morning, when the tempest drops,
At every cottage door mountainous heaps
Of snow lie drifted, that all entrance stops
Until the beesom and the shovel gain
The path, and leave a wall on either side.
The shepherd rambling valleys white and wide
With new sensations his old memory fills,
When hedges left at night, no more descried,
Are turned to one white sweep of curving hills,
And trees turned bushes half their bodies hide.

The boy that goes to fodder with surprise
Walks oer the gate he opened yesternight.
The hedges all have vanished from his eyes;
Een some tree tops the sheep could reach to bite.
The novel scene emboldens new delight,
And, though with cautious steps his sports begin,
He bolder shuffles the huge hills of snow,
Till down he drops and plunges to the chin,
And struggles much and oft escape to win –
Then turns and laughs but dare not further go;
For deep the grass and bushes lie below,
Where little birds that soon at eve went in
With heads tucked in their wings now pine for day
And little feel boys oer their heads can stray.

JOHN CLARE

Snowdrop

Now is the globe shrunk tight
Round the mouse's dulled wintering heart.
Weasel and crow, as if moulded in brass,
Move through an outer darkness
Not in their right minds,
With the other deaths. She, too, pursues her ends,
Brutal as the stars or this month,
Her pale head heavy as metal.

TED HUGHES

Soracte

Snow's on the fellside, look! How deep;
our wood's staggering under its weight.
The burns will be tonguetied
while frost lasts.

But we'll thaw out. Logs, logs for the hearth;
and don't spare my good whisky. No water, please.
Forget the weather. Elm and ash

will stop signalling
when this gale drops.
Why reckon? Why forecast? Pocket
whatever today brings,
and don't turn up your nose, it's childish,
at making love and dancing.
When you've my bare scalp, if you must, be glum.
Keep your date in the park while light's whispering.
Hunt her out, well wrapped up, hiding and giggling,
and get her bangle for a keepsake;
she won't make much fuss.

(*says Horace, more or less*)
BASIL BUNTING

The Twelve Days of Christmas

In England this memory game begins
'On the first day of Christmas my true love sent to me'.
The gifts eventually comprise:

A partridge in a pear tree, 2 turtle doves,
3 French hens, 4 colly birds, 5 gold rings,
6 geese a-laying, 7 swans a-swimming,
8 maids a-milking, 9 drummers drumming,
10 pipers piping, 11 ladies dancing,
12 lords a-leaping.

In Scotland the preamble runs 'The king sent his lady on
the first Yule day, a popingo-aye [parrot]; Wha learns my
carol and carries it away?' and the menagerie consists of:

3 partridges, 3 plovers, a goose that was grey,
3 starlings, 3 goldspinks, a bull that was brown,
3 ducks a-merry laying, 3 swans a-merry swimming,
an Arabian baboon, 3 hinds a-merry hunting,
3 maids a-merry dancing, 3 stalks o' merry corn.

In the west of France the list includes:

A good stuffing without bones, 2 breasts of veal,
3 joints of beef, 4 pigs' trotters, 5 legs of mutton,
6 partridges with cabbage, 7 spitted rabbits,
8 plates of salad, 9 dishes for a chapter of canons,
10 full casks, 11 beautiful full-breasted maidens,
12 musketeers with their swords.

TRAD.

Up in the Morning Early

Up in the morning's no for me,
  Up in the morning early;
When a' the hills are cover'd wi' snaw,
  I'm sure it's winter fairly.

Cold blaws the wind frae east to west,
  The drift is driving sairly;
Sae loud and shrill's I hear the blast,
  I'm sure it's winter fairly.

The birds sit chittering in the thorn,
  A' day they fare but sparely;
And lang's the night frae e'en to morn,
  I'm sure it's winter fairly.

Up in the morning's no for me,
  Up in the morning early;
When a' the hills are cover'd wi' snaw,
  I'm sure it's winter fairly.

ROBERT BURNS

A Wet Winter

from A Midsummer Night's Dream

Therefore the winds, piping to us in vain,
As in revenge have sucked up from the sea
Contagious fogs: which, falling in the land,
Hath every pelting river made so proud
That they have overborne their continents.
The ox hath therefore stretched his yoke in vain,
The ploughman lost his sweat, and the green corn
Hath rotted ere his youth attained a beard.
The fold stands empty in the drownèd field,
And crows are fatted with the murrion flock,
The nine men's morris is filled up with mud,
And the quaint mazes in the wanton green
For lack of tread are undistinguishable.

WILLIAM SHAKESPEARE

Winter

The boughs, the boughs are bare enough
But earth has never felt the snow.
Frost-furred our ivies are, and rough

With bills of rime the brambles shew.
The hoarse leaves crawl on hissing ground
Because the sighing wind is low.

But if the rain-blasts be unbound
And from dank feathers wring the drops
The clogged brook runs with choking sound

Kneading the mounded mire that stops
His channel under damming coats
Of foliage fallen in the copse.

A simple passage of weak notes
Is all the winter bird dare try
The bugle moon by daylight floats

So glassy white about the sky,
So like a berg of hyaline,
And pencilled blue so daintily,

I never saw her so divine
But through black branches, rarely drest
In scarves of silky shot and shine.

The webbèd and the watery west
Where yonder crimson fireball sits
Looks laid for feasting and for rest.

I see long reefs of violets
In beryl-covered fens so dim,
A gold-water Pactolus frets

Its brindled wharves and yellow brim,
The waxen colours weep and run
And slendering to his burning rim

Into the flat blue mist the sun
Drops out and all our day is done.

GERARD MANLEY HOPKINS

A Winter Night

It was a chilly winter's night;
   And frost was glitt'ring on the ground,
And evening stars were twinkling bright;
   And from the gloomy plain around
      Came no sound,
But where, within the wood-girt tow'r,
The churchbell slowly struck the hour;

As if that all of human birth
   Had risen to the final day,
And soaring from the wornout earth
   Were called in hurry and dismay,
      Far away;
And I alone of all mankind
Were left in loneliness behind.

WILLIAM BARNES

SPRING

April

from Prologue to The Canterbury Tales

Whan that Aprille with his shoures sote
The droghte of Marche hath perced to the rote,
And bathed every veyne in swich licour,
Of which vertu engendred is the flour;
Whan Zephirus eek with his swete breeth
Inspired hath in every holt and heeth
The tendre croppes, and the yonge sonne
Hath in the Ram his halfe cours y-ronne,
And smale fowles maken melodye,
That slepen al the night with open yë,
(So priketh hem nature in hir corages):
Than longen folk to goon on pilgrimages.

GEOFFREY CHAUCER

'Between March and April'

Bitwenë March and Avëril
When spray biginneth to springe,
The litel foul hath hirë wil
On hyrë lede to synge.
Ich live in love-longinge   5
For semeliest of allë thynge,
She may me blissë bringe,
Ich am in hire baundoun.
   An hendy hap Ichave y-hent,
   Ichot from hevene it is me sent,   10
   From allë wommen my love is lent
   And light on Alysoun.

On hew hire her is fair ynogh,
Hire browës broune, hire eyen blake,
With lufsom chere she on me logh,   15
With middel smal and wel y-make.
But she me wol to hirë take

1 Averil] *April*   2 spray] *twig* springe] *sprout*   3 foul]
bird hirë wil] *her desire*   4 on hyrë lede] *in her language*
6 semeliest] *fairest* thynge] *things, creatures*   8 boundoun]
power   9 *'a fair good fortune I have received'*   10 Ichot]
I know   11 lent] *gone*   12 light] *alighted*   13 on
hew] *in hue, colour* her] *hair*   15 lufsom chere] *lovely
expression* logh] *smiled*   16 middel smal] *slender waist*
well y-make] *well made*   17 but she] *unless she*

For to ben hire owen make,
Longe to live Ichulle forsake
And feyë falle adoun.   20
    An hendy, etc.

                                                    TRAD.

18   to ben] *to be*   make] *companion*   19   Ichulle forsake]
I will refuse   20   feyë] *doomed, dead*

The Cherry Trees

The cherry trees bend over and are shedding,
On the road where all that passed are dead,
Their petals, strewing the grass as for a wedding
This early May morn when there is none to wed.

EDWARD THOMAS

Death of a Naturalist

All year the flax-dam festered in the heart
Of the townland; green and heavy-headed
Flax had rotted there, weighted down by huge sods.
Daily it sweltered in the punishing sun.
Bubbles gargled delicately, bluebottles
Wove a strong gauze of sound around the smell.
There were dragonflies, spotted butterflies,
But best of all was the warm thick slobber
Of frogspawn that grew like clotted water
In the shade of the banks. Here, every spring
I would fill jampotfuls of the jellied
Specks to range on window-sills at home,
On shelves at school, and wait and watch until
The fattening dots burst into nimble-
Swimming tadpoles. Miss Walls would tell us how
The daddy frog was called a bullfrog
And how he croaked and how the mammy frog
Laid hundreds of little eggs and this was
Frogspawn. You could tell the weather by frogs too
For they were yellow in the sun and brown
In rain.

  Then one hot day when fields were rank
With cowdung in the grass the angry frogs
Invaded the flax-dam; I ducked through hedges
To a coarse croaking that I had not heard
Before. The air was thick with a bass chorus.
Right down the dam gross-bellied frogs were cocked

On sods; their loose necks pulsed like sails. Some hopped:
The slap and plop were obscene threats. Some sat
Poised like mud grenades, their blunt heads farting.
I sickened, turned, and ran. The great slime kings
Were gathered there for vengeance and I knew
That if I dipped my hand the spawn would clutch it.

SEAMUS HEANEY

First Sight of Spring

The hazel-blooms, in threads of crimson hue,
Peep through the swelling buds, foretelling Spring,
Ere yet a white-thorn leaf appears in view,
Or March finds throstles pleased enough to sing.
To the old touchwood tree woodpeckers cling
A moment, and their harsh-toned notes renew;
In happier mood, the stockdove claps his wing;
The squirrel sputters up the powdered oak,
With tail cocked o'er his head, and ears erect,
Startled to hear the woodman's understroke;
And with the courage which his fears collect,
He hisses fierce half malice and half glee,
Leaping from branch to branch about the tree,
In winter's foliage, moss and lichens, deckt.

JOHN CLARE

Gorse Fires

Cattle out of their byres are dungy still, lambs
Have stepped from last year as from an enclosure.
Five or six men stand gazing at a rusty tractor
Before carrying implements to separate fields.

I am travelling from one April to another.
It is the same train between the same embankments.
Gorse fires are smoking, but primroses burn
And celandines and white may and gorse flowers.

MICHAEL LONGLEY

Home-Thoughts, from Abroad

I

Oh, to be in England
Now that April's there,
And whoever wakes in England
Sees, some morning, unaware,
That the lowest boughs and the brushwood sheaf
Round the elm-tree bole are in tiny leaf,
While the chaffinch sings on the orchard bough
In England – now!

II

And after April, when May follows,
And the whitethroat builds, and all the swallows!
Hark, where my blossomed pear-tree in the hedge
Leans to the field and scatters on the clover
Bossoms and dewdrops – at the bent spray's edge –
That's the wise thrush; he sings each song twice over,
Lest you should think he never could recapture
The first fine careless rapture!
And though the fields look rough with hoary dew
All will be gay when noontide wakes anew
The buttercups, the little children's dower
– Far brighter than this gaudy melon-flower!

ROBERT BROWNING

'I sing of a maiden'

I sing of a maiden
That is makeles:
King of alle kinges
To here sone she ches.

He cam also stille
Ther his moder was,
As dew in Aprille
That falleth on the grass.

He cam also stille
To his moderes bowr,
As dew in Aprille
That falleth on the flowr.

He cam also stille
Ther his moder lay,
As dew in Aprille
That falleth on the spray.

Moder and maiden
Was never non but she;
Well may swich a lady
Godes moder be.

TRAD.

In the Fields

Lord, when I look at lovely things which pass,
   Under old trees the shadows of young leaves
Dancing to please the wind along the grass,
    Or the gold stillness of the August sun on the
        August sheaves;
Can I believe there is a heavenlier world than this?
   And if there is
Will the strange heart of any everlasting thing
   Bring me these dreams that take my breath away?
They come at evening with the home-flying rooks
    and the scent of hay,
    Over the fields. They come in Spring.

CHARLOTTE MEW

June Thunder

The Junes were free and full, driving through tiny
Roads, the mudguards brushing the cowparsley,
Through fields of mustard and under boldly embattled
     Mays and chestnuts

Or between beeches verdurous and voluptuous
Or where broom and gorse beflagged the chalkland –
All the flare and gusto of the unenduring
     Joys of a season

Now returned but I note as more appropriate
To the maturer mood impending thunder
With an indigo sky and the garden hushed except for
     The treetops moving.

Then the curtains in my room blow suddenly inward,
The shrubbery rustles, birds fly heavily homeward,
The white flowers fade to nothing on the trees and rain comes
     Down like a dropscene.

Now there comes the catharsis, the cleansing downpour
Breaking the blossoms of our overdated fancies
Our old sentimentality and whimsicality
     Loves of the morning.

Blackness at half-past eight, the night's precursor,
Clouds like falling masonry and lightning's lavish
Annunciation, the sword of the mad archangel
     Flashed from the scabbard.

[54]

If only you would come and dare the crystal
Rampart of rain and the bottomless moat of thunder,
If only now you would come I should be happy
  Now if now only.

                              LOUIS MACNEICE

Lines Written in Early Spring

I heard a thousand blended notes,
While in a grove I sate reclined,
In that sweet mood when pleasant thoughts
Bring sad thoughts to the mind.

To her fair words did Nature link
The human soul that through me ran;
And much it grieved my heart to think
What man has made of man.

Through primrose tufts, in that green bower,
The periwinkle trailed its wreaths;
And 'tis my faith that every flower
Enjoys the air it breathes.

The birds around me hopped and played,
Their thoughts I cannot measure: –
But the least motion which they made,
It seemed a thrill of pleasure.

The budding twigs spread out their fan,
To catch the breezy air;
And I must think, do all I can,
That there was pleasure there.

If this belief from heaven be sent,
If such be Nature's holy plan,
Have I not reason to lament
What man has made of man?

WILLIAM WORDSWORTH

'Loveliest of trees, the cherry now'

from A Shropshire Lad

Loveliest of trees, the cherry now
Is hung with bloom along the bough,
And stands about the woodland ride
Wearing white for Eastertide.

Now, of my threescore years and ten,
Twenty will not come again,
And take from seventy springs a score,
It only leaves me fifty more.

And since to look at things in bloom
Fifty springs are little room,
About the woodlands I will go
To see the cherry hung with snow.

A. E. HOUSMAN

May

O! the month of May, the merry month of May,
  So frolic, so gay, and so green, so green, so green!
O! and then did I unto my true Love say,
  Sweet Peg, thou shalt be my Summer's Queen.

Now the nightingale, the pretty nightingale,
  The sweetest singer in all the forest's choir,
Entreats thee, sweet Peggy, to hear thy true Love's tale:
  Lo! yonder she sitteth, her breast against a briar.

But O! I spy the cuckoo, the cuckoo, the cuckoo;
  See where she sitteth; come away, my joy:
Come away, I prithee, I do not like the cuckoo
  Should sing where my Peggy and I kiss and toy.

O! the month of May, the merry month of May,
  So frolic, so gay, and so green, so green, so green!
And then did I unto my true Love say,
  Sweet Peg, thou shalt be my Summer's Queen.

THOMAS DEKKER

Nature and Man

from Queen Mab

                Look on yonder earth:
The golden harvests spring; the unfailing sun
Sheds light and life; the fruits, the flowers, the trees,
Arise in due succession; all things speak
Peace, harmony, and love. The universe,
In nature's silent eloquence, declares
That all fulfil the works of love and joy, –
All but the outcast man.

PERCY BYSSHE SHELLEY

Neighbours

That spring was late. We watched the sky
and studied charts for shouldering isobars.
Birds were late to pair. Crows drank from the lamb's eye.

Over Finland small birds fell: song-thrushes
steering north, smudged signatures on light,
migrating warblers, nightingales.

Wing-beats failed over fjords, each lung a sip of gall.
Children were warned of their dangerous beauty.
Milk was spilt in Poland. Each quarrel

the blowback from some old story,
a mouthful of bitter air from the Ukraine
brought by the wind out of its box of sorrows.

This spring a lamb sips caesium on a Welsh hill.
A child, lifting her face to drink the rain,
takes into her blood the poisoned arrow.

Now we are all neighbourly, each little town
in Europe twinned to Chernobyl, each heart
with the burnt fireman, the child on the Moscow train.

In the democracy of the virus and the toxin
we wait. We watch for bird migrations,
one bird returning with green in its voice,

glasnost,
golau glas,
a first break of blue.

GILLIAN CLARKE

golau glas] *blue light*

The Night Song

Sung at Padstow on May Day

Unite, unite, let us all unite,
For Summer is a-come unto day
And whither we are going we will all unite
    On the merry morning of May.

The young men of Padstow, they might if they would,
For Summer is a-come unto day.
They might have built a ship and gilded her with gold,
    On the merry morning of May.

The maidens of Padstow, they might if they would,
For Summer is a-come unto day.
They might have made a garland of the white rose and the red
    On the merry morning of May.

Up Merry Spring, and up the merry ring,
For Summer is a-come unto day!
How happy are those little birds that merrily do sing
    On the merry morning of May!

TRAD.

Nuts in May

May come up with bird-din
And May come up with sun-dint,
May come up with water-wheels
    And May come up with iris.

In the sun-peppered meadow the shepherds are old,
Their flutes are broken and their tales are told,
And their ears are deaf when the guns unfold
The new philosophy over the wold.

May come up with pollen of death,
May come up with cordite,
May come up with a chinagraph
    And May come up with a stopwatch.

In the high court of heaven Their tail-feathers shine
With cowspit and bullspit and spirits of wine,
They know no pity, being divine,
And They give no quarter to thine or mine.

May come up with Very lights,
May come up with duty,
May come up with a bouncing cheque,
    An acid-drop and a bandage.

Yes, angels are frigid and shepherds are dumb,
There is no holy water when the enemy come,
The trees are askew and the skies are a-hum
And you have to keep mum and go to it and die for your
    life and keep mum.

May come up with fiddle-bows,
May come up with blossom,
May come up the same again,
    The same again but different.

LOUIS MACNEICE

The Passionate Shepherd to His Love

Come live with me, and be my love,
And we will all the pleasures prove,
That valleys, groves, hills, and fields,
Woods, or steepy mountain yields.

And we will sit upon the rocks,
Seeing the shepherds feed their flocks,
By shallow rivers to whose falls
Melodious birds sing madrigals.

And I will make thee beds of roses,
And a thousand fragrant posies,
A cap of flowers, and a kirtle,
Embroidered all with leaves of myrtle;

A gown made of the finest wool,
Which from our pretty lambs we pull;
Fair linèd slippers for the cold,
With buckles of the purest gold;

A belt of straw and ivy buds,
With coral clasps and amber studs:
And if these pleasures may thee move,
Come live with me, and be my love.

kirtle] *gown or shirt*

The shepherds' swains shall dance and sing
For thy delight each May morning.
If these delights thy mind may move,
Then live with me, and be my love.

CHRISTOPHER MARLOWE

Spring in Belfast

Walking among my own this windy morning
In a tide of sunlight between shower and shower,
I resume my old conspiracy with the wet
Stone and the unwieldy images of the squinting heart.
Once more, as before, I remember not to forget.

There is a perverse pride in being on the side
Of the fallen angels and refusing to get up.
We could *all* be saved by keeping an eye on the hill
At the top of every street, for there it is,
Eternally, if irrelevantly, visible –

But yield instead to the humorous formulae,
The spurious mystery in the knowing nod;
Or we keep sullen silence in light and shade,
Rehearsing our astute salvations under
The cold gaze of a sanctimonious God.

One part of my mind must learn to know its place.
The things that happen in the kitchen houses
And echoing back streets of this desperate city
Should engage more than my casual interest,
Exact more interest than my casual pity.

DEREK MAHON

'Sumer is icumen in'

Sumer is icumen in,
Loud sing cuckoo!
Groweth seed and bloweth mead
And springeth the wood now.
Sing cuckoo!

Ewe bleateth after lamb,
Cow loweth after calf,
Bullock starteth, buck farteth,
Merry sing cuckoo!

Cuckoo, cuckoo!
Well singest thou cuckoo,
Nor cease thou never now!

Sing cuckoo now, sing cuckoo!
Sing cuckoo, sing cuckoo now!

TRAD.

To Violets

1. Welcome Maids of Honour,
      You doe bring
      In the Spring;
   And wait upon her.

2. She has Virgins many,
      Fresh and faire;
      Yet you are
   More sweet than any.

3. Y'are the Maiden Posies,
      And so grac't
      To be plac't
   'Fore Damask Roses.

4. Yet though thus respected,
      By and by
      Ye doe lie,
   Poore Girles, neglected.

ROBERT HERRICK

The Trees

The trees are coming into leaf
Like something almost being said;
The recent buds relax and spread,
Their greenness is a kind of grief.

Is it that they are born again
And we grow old? No, they die too.
Their yearly trick of looking new
Is written down in rings of grain.

Yet still the unresting castles thresh
In fullgrown thickness every May.
Last year is dead, they seem to say,
Begin afresh, afresh, afresh.

PHILIP LARKIN

The Tuft of Violets

Our solitary larch
Spread her green silk against the south,
When late-relenting March
Ended the sowing-time of welcome drouth;
And from the bank beneath
Sheltered by budding hedge and bowing tree,
A moist delicious breath
Of rainy violets came out to me.

There was the healthy mass
Of dark delightful leaves, with their own breath
Of silvan moss and grass;
But all among and over them there went

The sweetness lovers know,
And age will pause upon, while time returns,
And earlier violets grow
In a lost kingdom where no creature mourns.

From high above my head
The mated missel-thrush was singing proudly,
And through that dusky bed
The light-reflecting bee rejoicing loudly,
Kissing each modest face,
Sang to them well how beautiful they were,
Who in that slight embrace
Let fall upon the green a little tear.

Time ceased, as if the spring
Had been eternity; I had no age;
The purple and the wing
That visited and hymned it, were a page
Royally dyed, written in gold;
Royal with truth, for ever springing;
For ever, as of old,
The sunlight and the darkness and the singing.

RUTH PITTER

A Wood Coming into Leaf

From the first to the second

Warily, from the tip to the palm

Third leaf (the blackthorn done)

From the fourth to the fifth and
(Larix, Castanea, Fraxinus, Tilia)

Thaw taps, groping in stumps,
frost like an adder easing away

The sixth to the seventh (plums conceive
a knobble in a stone within a blossom)

Ushers the next by the thumbs to the next . . .

A thirty-first, a thirty-second

A greenwood through a blackwood
passes (like the moon's halves
meet and go behind themselves)

And you and I, quarter-alight, our boots in shadow

Birch, oak, rowan, ash
chinese-whispering the change.

ALICE OSWALD

Young Lambs

The spring is coming by a many signs;
   The trays are up, the hedges broken down,
That fenced the haystack, and the remnant shines
   Like some old antique fragment weathered brown.
And where suns peep, in every sheltered place,
   The little early buttercups unfold
A glittering star or two – till many trace
   The edges of the blackthorn clumps in gold.
And then a little lamb bolts up behind
   The hill and wags his tail to meet the yoe,
And then another, sheltered from the wind,
   Lies all his length as dead – and lets me go
Close bye and never stirs but baking lies,
   With legs stretched out as though he could not rise.

JOHN CLARE

SUMMER

Adlestrop

Yes. I remember Adlestrop –
The name, because one afternoon
Of heat the express-train drew up there
Unwontedly. It was late June.

The steam hissed. Someone cleared his throat.
No one left and no one came
On the bare platform. What I saw
Was Adlestrop – only the name

And willows, willow-herb, and grass,
And meadowsweet, and haycocks dry,
No whit less still and lonely fair
Than the high cloudlets in the sky.

And for that minute a blackbird sang
Close by, and round him, mistier,
Farther and farther, all the birds
Of Oxfordshire and Gloucestershire.

EDWARD THOMAS

Cowslips and Larks

I hear it said yon land is poor,
In spite of those rich cowslips there –
And all the singing larks it shoots
To heaven from the cowslips' roots.
But I, with eyes that beauty find,
And music ever in my mind,
Feed my thoughts well upon that grass
Which starves the horse, the ox, and ass.
So here I stand, two miles to come
To Shapwick and my ten-days-home,
Taking my summer's joy, although
The distant clouds are dark and low,
And comes a storm that, fierce and strong,
Has brought the Mendip Hills along:
Those hills that, when the light is there,
Are many a sunny mile from here.

W. H. DAVIES

Cut Grass

Cut grass lies frail:
Brief is the breath
Mown stalks exhale.
Long, long the death

It dies in the white hours
Of young-leafed June
With chestnut flowers,
With hedges snowlike strewn,

White lilac bowed,
Lost lanes of Queen Anne's lace,
And that high-builded cloud
Moving at summer's pace.

PHILIP LARKIN

Dew

The tense stand-off
of summer's end,
the touchy fuse-wire
of parched grass,
tapers of bulrush and reed,
any tree
a primed mortar
of tinder, one spark
enough to trigger
a march on the moor
by ranks of flame.

Dew enters the field
under cover of night,
tending the weary and sapped,
lifting its thimble of drink
to the lips of a leaf,
to the stoat's tongue,
trimming a length of barbed-wire fence
with liquid gems, here
where bog-cotton
flags its surrender
or carries its torch
for the rain.

Then dawn, when sunrise
plants its fire-star
in each drop, ignites
each trembling eye.

SIMON ARMITAGE

[80]

For Summer

The lie is light over your heart.
You will do nothing about it.
The swallows are chattering
around the house. All night
you sweat it out waiting for a breeze
to collapse you to sleep.

You lay down in front of your door,
your head pointing north, but
none of the other cardinal points
creep into your body. Your ears,
loosened with olive oil, tune into
difficult stars, loud and hot.

Summer is going. You are already
running into the first snowflake,
mouth open to taste it, primed
to ingest all the weathers.

JO SHAPCOTT

Heatwave

It was August
when we saw the man
with an iguana on his shoulder
walk up from the wharf.

No mirage –
the huge lizard
unblinking
in outlandish light

while downwind
the lions at Colchester zoo
were fed lumps of ice
flavoured with blood.

PAULINE STAINER

Heliotropical

Brightness burns midsummer's eve
fires to air: they crackle, invisible.

At midnight, the sun glides into reverse
like Anna backwards, a god having second thoughts.

It looks easy, but hurts.
I'm strung out on a fifty-foot shadow,

up to my knees in dandelion clocks
which glow like liquid worlds of sleep.

A dip below the surface of sleep
and then hours of ecstatic frenetic.

Light pumps into the room, pumps into me,
leaving nothing to fill.

My heart bursts with joy, every cell,
and the light comes still.

LAVINIA GREENLAW

High Summer

I never wholly feel that summer is high,
However green the trees, or loud the birds,
However movelessly eye-winking herds
Stand in field ponds, or under large trees lie,
Till I do climb all cultured pastures by,
That hedged by hedgerows studiously fretted trim,
Smile like a lady's face with lace laced prim,
And on some moor or hill that seeks the sky
Lonely and nakedly, – utterly lie down,
And feel the sunshine throbbing on body and limb,
My drowsy brain in pleasant drunkenness swim,
Each rising thought sink back and dreamily drown,
Smiles creep o'er my face, and smother my lips, and cloy,
Each muscle sink to itself, and separately enjoy.

EBENEZER JONES

'In somer, when the shawes be sheyne'

from The Ballad of Robyn Hode and the Munke

In somer, when the shawes be sheyne
    And leves be large and long,
Hit is full mery in feyre foreste
    To here the foulys song;

To se the dere draw to the dale
    And leve the hilles hee,
And shadow hem in the leves grene
    Vnder the grene-wode tre . . .

TRAD.

John Barleycorn

There were three men came out of the west
Their fortunes for to try,
And these three men made a solemn vow
John Barleycorn should die.

They've ploughed, they've sown, they've harrowed him in,
Throw'd clods upon his head,
And these three men made a solemn vow
John Barleycorn was dead.

They've let him lie for a very long time
Till the rain from heaven did fall,
Then little Sir John sprung up his head
And soon amazed them all.

They've let him stand till Midsummer Day
Till he looked both pale and wan,
And little Sir John's grown a long, long beard
And so become a man.

They've hired men with their scythes so sharp
To cut him off at the knee,
They've rolled and tied him by the waist,
Serving him most barb'rously.

They've hired men with their sharp pitch forks
Who pricked him to the heart,
And the loader he served him worse than that
For he's bound him to the cart.

They've wheeled him round and around the field
Till they came unto the barn
And there they've made a solemn mow
Of poor John Barleycorn.

They've hired men with the crabtree sticks
To cut him skin from bone,
And the miller he has served him worse than that
For he's ground him between two stones.

Here's little Sir John in the nut brown bowl
And here's brandy in the glass,
And little Sir John in the nut brown bowl
Proved the strongest man at last

For the huntsman he can't hunt the fox
And so loudly blow his horn
And the tinker he can't mend kettles nor pots
Without a little barleycorn.

TRAD.

'Now welcome, somer, with thy sonne softe'

from The Parliament of Fowls

Now welcome, somer, with thy sonne softe,
That hast this wintres wedres overshake,
And driven away the longe nyghtes blake!

Saynt Valentyn, that art ful hy on-lofte,
Thus syngen smale foules for thy sake:
Now welcome, somer, with thy sonne softe,
That hast this wintres wedres overshake.

Wel han they cause for to gladen ofte,
Sith ech of hem recovered hath hys make;
Ful blissful mowe they synge when they wake:
Now welcome, somer, with thy sonne softe
That hast this wintres wedres overshake
And driven away the longe nyghtes blake!

GEOFFREY CHAUCER

Out of Time

It is a formal and deserted garden
With many a flower bed and winding path.
A cupid stands and draws a bow at venture
Upon a marble bath.

All round his feet the eager ivy grows,
Stretches upon the stone, above the ground,
And in the ivy flowers the busy bee
Makes a melodious sound.

The air is ponderous with summer scents
And still it lies upon the garden all
As still and secret as it stayed upon
A funeral.

The sun shines brightly in the upper air
And casts his beams upon the garden grass.
There spilled they lie a carpet of dull gold
Where shadows pass.

The garden gives to these primeval beams
That strew its floor a plastered yellow tone
As of too mellow sunshine that brings on
A thunder stone.

It is an ominous enchanted garden
That can transmogrify the healthful rays,
Can hold and make them an essential part
Of unquiet days.

Ah me, the unquiet days they tread me down,
The hours and minutes beat upon my head.
I have spent here the time of three men's lives
And am not dead.

And even as I count the days that pass
I lose the total and begin again.
It is an evil garden out of Time
A place of pain.

STEVIE SMITH

Poppies in July

Little poppies, little hell flames,
Do you do no harm?

You flicker. I cannot touch you.
I put my hands among the flames. Nothing burns.

And it exhausts me to watch you
Flickering like that, wrinkly and clear red, like the skin of
    a mouth.

A mouth just bloodied.
Little bloody skirts!

There are fumes that I cannot touch.
Where are your opiates, your nauseous capsules?

If I could bleed or sleep! –
If my mouth could marry a hurt like that!

Or your liquors seep to me, in this glass capsule,
Dulling and stilling.

But colorless. Colorless.

SYLVIA PLATH

The School Boy

I love to rise in a summer morn,
When the birds sing on every tree;
The distant huntsman winds his horn,
And the sky-lark sings with me.
O! what sweet company.

But to go to school in a summer morn
O! it drives all joy away;
Under a cruel eye outworn,
The little ones spend the day,
In sighing and dismay.

Ah! then at times I drooping sit,
And spend many an anxious hour.
Nor in my book can I take delight,
Nor sit in learning's bower,
Worn thro' with the dreary shower

How can the bird that is born for joy,
Sit in a cage and sing.
How can a child when fears annoy,
But droop his tender wing,
And forget his youthful spring.

O! father and mother, if buds are nip'd,
And blossoms blown away,
And if the tender plants are strip'd
Of their joy in the springing day,
By sorrow and cares dismay,

How shall the summer arise in joy
Or the summer fruits appear
Or how shall we gather what griefs destroy
Or bless the mellowing year,
When the blasts of winter appear.

WILLIAM BLAKE

Strawberries

There were never strawberries
like the ones we had
that sultry afternoon
sitting on the step
of the open french window
facing each other
your knees held in mine
the blue plates in our laps
the strawberries glistening
in the hot sunlight
we dipped them in sugar
looking at each other
not hurrying the feast
for one to come
the empty plates
laid on the stone together
with the two forks crossed
and I bent towards you
sweet in that air
in my arms
abandoned like a child
from your eager mouth
the taste of strawberries
in my memory
lean back again
let me love you

let the sun beat
on our forgetfulness
one hour of all
the heat intense
and summer lightning
on the Kilpatrick hills

let the storm wash the plates

EDWIN MORGAN

Summer

'For months the heat of love has kept me marching'
                    – ROBERT LOWELL

I snap my boy's bow
in the morning, wash his stiffy at night, blow my brains out
with music, anything from 'Ballade von der sexuellen
    Hörigkeit'
to 'Sexual Healing'. *Je te veux.*

The vaunted sod
under my feet is rolled up like a piece of turf or a blanket
in my grenadier's knapsack, along with a toothbrush
and near-pristine candle end.

A loose cannon
combing the phone book and the small ads for friendly
    addresses,
a nine-year-old regaling my parents with the Roget's
entry on sex. 'Anyone for urolagnia?'

Pulling on the telephone
like a bottle, a permanent unendurable fluttering in the
    diaphragm,
dogdays, the sighs of the Pléiade, planets in love,
mouthsounds, genie, come . . .

Hyde Park
twenty-four hours apart, Baker Street from the top of a
    bus,
the curve of the overground train past your house,
past mine, nowhere to grip in the slippery city.

The London plane tree by my window
hangs its green leatherette sleeves, exhausted by a hard
    May.
My varsity jacket. The sky between leaves is the brightest
    thing in nature,
Virginia Woolf told the inquiring Rupert Brooke. Whatever.

MICHAEL HOFMANN

Summer Dawn

Pray but one prayer for me 'twixt thy closed lips,
Think but one thought of me up in the stars.
   The summer night waneth, the morning light slips,
Faint & grey 'twixt the leaves of the aspen, betwixt the
    cloud-bars,
That are patiently waiting there for the dawn:
   Patient and colourless, though Heaven's gold
Waits to float through them along with the sun.
Far out in the meadows, above the young corn,
   The heavy elms wait, and restless and cold
The uneasy wind rises; the roses are dun;
Through the long twilight they pray for the dawn.
Round the lone house in the midst of the corn.
Speak but one word to me over the corn,
Over the tender, bow'd locks of the corn.

WILLIAM MORRIS

A Summer Night

to Geoffrey Hoyland

Out on the lawn I lie in bed,
Vega conspicuous overhead
    In the windless nights of June,
As congregated leaves complete
Their day's activity; my feet
    Point to the rising moon.

Lucky, this point in time and space
Is chosen as my working-place,
    Where the sexy airs of summer,
The bathing hours and the bare arms,
The leisured drives through a land of farms
    Are good to a newcomer.

Equal with colleagues in a ring
I sit on each calm evening
    Enchanted as the flowers
The opening light draws out of hiding
With all its gradual dove-like pleading,
    Its logic and its powers:

That later we, though parted then,
May still recall these evenings when
    Fear gave his watch no look;
The lion griefs loped from the shade
And on our knees their muzzles laid,
    And Death put down his book.

Now north and south and east and west
Those I love lie down to rest;
    The moon looks on them all,
The healers and the brilliant talkers,
The eccentrics and the silent walkers,
    The dumpy and the tall.

She climbs the European sky,
Churches and power-stations lie
    Alike among earth's fixtures:
Into the galleries she peers
And blankly as a butcher stares
    Upon the marvellous pictures.

To gravity attentive, she
Can notice nothing here, though we
    Whom hunger does not move,
From gardens where we feel secure
Look up and with a sigh endure
    The tyrannies of love:

And, gentle, do not care to know,
Where Poland draws her eastern bow,
    What violence is done,
Nor ask what doubtful act allows
Our freedom in this English house,
    Our picnics in the sun.

Soon, soon, through dykes of our content
The crumpling flood will force a rent
    And, taller than a tree,
Hold sudden death before our eyes
Whose river dreams long hid the size
    And vigours of the sea.

But when the waters make retreat
And through the black mud first the wheat
   In shy green stalks appears,
When stranded monsters gasping lie,
And sounds of riveting terrify
   Their whorled unsubtle ears,

May these delights we dread to lose,
This privacy, need no excuse
   But to that strength belong,
As through a child's rash happy cries
The drowned parental voices rise
   In unlamenting song.

After discharges of alarm
All unpredicted let them calm
   The pulse of nervous nations,
Forgive the murderer in his glass,
Tough in their patience to surpass
   The tigress her swift motions.

                  W. H. AUDEN

Summer Shower

A drop fell on the apple tree,
Another on the roof;
A half a dozen kissed the eaves,
And made the gables laugh.

A few went out to help the brook,
That went to help the sea.
Myself conjectured, Were they pearls,
What necklaces could be!

The dust replaced in hoisted roads,
The birds jocoser sung;
The sunshine threw his hat away,

The orchards spangles hung.
The breezes brought dejected lutes,
And bathed them in the glee;
The East put out a single flag,
And signed the fête away.

EMILY DICKINSON

Thistles

Against the rubber tongues of cows and the hoeing hands
  of men
Thistles spike the summer air
Or crackle open under a blue-black pressure.

Every one a revengeful burst
Of resurrection, a grasped fistful
Of splintered weapons and Icelandic frost thrust up

From the underground stain of a decayed Viking.
They are like pale hair and the gutturals of dialects.
Every one manages a plume of blood.

Then they grow grey, like men.
Mown down, it is a feud. Their sons appear,
Stiff with weapons, fighting back over the same ground.

TED HUGHES

Threshing Morning

On an apple-ripe September morning
Through the mist-chill fields I went
With a pitchfork on my shoulder
Less for use than for devilment.

The threshing mill was set-up, I knew,
In Cassidy's haggard last night,
And we owed them a day at the threshing
Since last year. O it was delight

To be paying bills of laughter
And chaffy gossip in kind
With work thrown in to ballast
The fantasy-soaring mind.

As I crossed the wooden bridge I wondered
As I looked into the drain
If ever a summer morning should find me
Shovelling up eels again.

And I thought of the wasps' nest in the bank
And how I got chased one day
Leaving the drag and the scraw-knife behind,
How I covered my face with hay.

The wet leaves of the cocksfoot
Polished my boots as I
Went round by the glistening bog-holes
Lost in unthinking joy.

I'll be carrying bags today, I mused,
The best job at the mill
With plenty of time to talk of our loves
As we wait for the bags to fill . . .

Maybe Mary might call round . . .
And then I came to the haggard gate,
And I knew as I entered that I had come
Through fields that were part of no earthly estate.

PATRICK KAVANAGH

Trees Be Company

When zummer's burnen het's a-shed
Upon the droopen grasses head,
A-drevèn under sheädy leaves
The workvo'k in their snow-white sleeves,
We then mid yearn to clim' the height,
    Where thorns be white, above the vern;
An' air do turn the zunsheen's might
      To softer light too weak to burn –
        On woodless downs we mid be free,
        But lowland trees be company.

Though downs mid show a wider view
O' green a-reachen into blue
Than roads a-winden in the glen,
An' ringen wi' the sounds o' men;
The thissle's crown o' red an' blue
    In Fall's cwold dew do wither brown,
An' larks come down 'ithin the lew,
      As storms do brew, an' skies do frown –
        An' though the down do let us free,
        The lowland trees be company.

Where birds do zing, below the zun,
In trees above the blue-smok'd tun,
An' sheädes o' stems do overstratch
The mossy path 'ithin the hatch;
If leaves be bright up over head,
    When Mäy do shed its glitt'ren light;
Or, in the blight o'Fall, do spread

A yollow bed avore our zight –
    Whatever season it mid be,
    The trees be always company.

When dusky night do nearly hide
The path along the hedge's zide,
An' daylight's hwomely sounds be still
But sounds o'water at the mill;
Then if noo feäce we long'd to greet
    Could come to meet our lwonesome treäce;
Or if noo peäce o' weary veet,
    However fleet, could reach its pleäce –
    However lwonesome we mid be,
    The trees would still be company.

                    WILLIAM BARNES

The Trees of Ireland

from Sweeney Astray

The bushy leafy oak tree
is highest in the wood,
the forking shoots of hazel
hide sweet hazel-nuts.

The alder is my darling,
all thornless in the gap,
some milk of human kindness
coursing in its sap.

The blackthorn is a jaggy creel
stippled with dark sloes;
green watercress in thatch on wells
where the drinking blackbird goes.

Sweetest of the leafy stalks,
the vetches strew the pathway;
the oyster-grass is my delight
and the wild strawberry.

Low-set clumps of apple trees
drum down fruit when shaken;
scarlet berries clot like blood
on mountain rowan.

Briars curl in sideways,
arch a stickle back,
draw blood and curl up innocent
to sneak the next attack.

The yew tree in each churchyard
wraps night in its dark hood.
Ivy is a shadowy
genius of the wood.

Holly rears its windbreak,
a door in winter's face;
life-blood on a spear-shaft
darkens the grain of ash.

Birch tree, smooth and blessed,
delicious to the breeze,
high twigs plait and crown it
the queen of trees.

The aspen pales
and whispers, hesitates:
a thousand frightened scuts
race in its leaves.

But what disturbs me the most
in the leafy wood
is the to and fro and to and fro
of an oak rod.

SEAMUS HEANEY

The Way Through the Woods

They shut the road through the woods
Seventy years ago.
Weather and rain have undone it again,
And now you would never know
There was once a road through the woods
Before they planted the trees.
It is underneath the coppice and heath
And the thin anemones.
Only the keeper sees
That, where the ring-dove broods,
And the badgers roll at ease,
There was once a road through the woods.

Yet, if you enter the woods
Of a summer evening late,
When the night-air cools on the trout-ringed pools
Where the otter whistles his mate,
(They fear not men in the woods,
Because they see so few.)
You will hear the beat of a horse's feet,
And the swish of a skirt in the dew,
Steadily cantering through
The misty solitudes,
As though they perfectly knew
The old lost road through the woods . . .
But there is no road through the woods.

RUDYARD KIPLING

'When summer's end is nighing'

from Last Poems

When summer's end is nighing
   And skies at evening cloud,
I muse on change and fortune
   And all the feats I vowed
   When I was young and proud.

The weathercock at sunset
   Would lose the slanted ray,
And I would climb the beacon
   That looked to Wales away
   And saw the last of day.

From hill and cloud and heaven
   The hues of evening died;
Night welled through lane and hollow
   And hushed the countryside,
   But I had youth and pride.

And I with earth and nightfall
   In converse high would stand,
Late, till the west was ashen
   And darkness hard at hand,
   And the eye lost the land.

The year might age, and cloudy
   The lessening day might close,
But air of other summers
   Breathed from beyond the snows,
   And I had hope of those.

They came and were and are not
   And come no more anew;
And all the years and seasons
   That ever can ensue
   Must now be worse and few.

So here's an end of roaming
   On eves when autumn nighs:
The ear too fondly listens
   For summer's parting sighs,
   And then the heart replies.

A. E. HOUSMAN

AUTUMN

Alcaic

Out in the deep wood, silence and darkness fall,
down through the wet leaves comes the October mist;
   no sound, but only a blackbird scolding,
      making the mist and the darkness listen.

PETER LEVI

Autumn

I love to see, when leaves depart,
The clear anatomy arrive,
Winter, the paragon of art,
That kills all forms of life and feeling
Save what is pure and will survive.

Already now the clanging chains
Of geese are harnessed to the moon:
Stripped are the great sun-clouding planes:
And the dark pines, their own revealing,
Let in the needles of the noon.

Strained by the gale the olives whiten
Like hoary wrestlers bent with toil
And, with the vines, their branches lighten
To brim our vats where summer lingers
In the red froth and sun-gold oil.

Soon on our hearth's reviving pyre
Their rotted stems will crumble up:
And like a ruby, panting fire,
The grape will redden on your fingers
Through the lit crystal of the cup.

ROY CAMPBELL

Autumn

The sun shines on my desk.
Such joy, such joy it is
to work as if at music
on such clear autumn days.

When the rowans all in red
bend over water and
above the arranged dead
there is no breath of wind,

and eternity is this
tranquillity and poise
of orange-coloured trees
and flame-red bare displays

as if a visible fire
were an image of itself
both fact and its idea
trembling in double leaf.

IAN CRICHTON SMITH

Autumn Nature Notes 1

The Laburnum top is silent, quite still
In the afternoon yellow September sunlight,
A few leaves yellowing, all its seeds fallen.

Till the goldfinch comes, with a twitching chirrup,
A suddenness, a startlement, at a branch-end.
Then sleek as a lizard, and alert, and abrupt
She enters the thickness, and a machine starts up
Of chitterings, and a tremor of wings, and trillings –
The whole tree trembles and thrills.
It is the engine of her family.
She stokes it full, then flirts out to a branch-end
Showing her barred face identity mask

Then with eerie delicate whistle-chirrup whisperings
She launches away, towards the infinite

And the laburnum subsides to empty.

TED HUGHES

Autumn on the Land

A man, a field, silence – what is there to say?
He lives, he moves, and the October day
Burns slowly down
               History is made
Elsewhere; the hours forfeit to time's blade
Don't matter here. The leaves large and small,
Shed by the branches, unlamented fall
About his shoulders. You may look in vain
Through the eyes' window; on his meagre hearth
The thin, shy soul has not begun its reign
Over the darkness. Beauty, love and mirth
And joy are strangers there.
                    You must revise
Your bland philosophy of nature, earth
Has of itself no power to make men wise.

R. S. THOMAS

Autumn Song

from Twelve Songs

Now the leaves are falling fast,
Nurse's flowers will not last,
Nurses to their graves are gone,
But the prams go rolling on.

Whispering neighbours left and right
Daunt us from our true delight,
Able hands are forced to freeze
Derelict on lonely knees.

Close behind us on our track,
Dead in hundreds cry Alack,
Arms raised stiffly to reprove
In false attitudes of love.

Scrawny through a plundered wood,
Trolls run scolding for their food,
Owl and nightingale are dumb,
And the angel will not come.

Clear, unscaleable, ahead
Rise the Mountains of Instead,
From whose cold cascading streams
None may drink except in dreams.

W. H. AUDEN

Bavarian Gentians

Not every man has gentians in his house
in soft September, at slow, sad Michaelmas.

Bavarian gentians, big and dark, only dark
darkening the day-time torch-like with the smoking
   blueness of Pluto's gloom,
ribbed and torch-like, with their blaze of darkness spread
   blue
down flattening into points, flattened under the sweep
   of white day,
torch-flower of the blue-smoking darkness, Pluto's
   dark-blue daze,
black lamps from the halls of Dis, burning dark blue,
giving off darkness, blue darkness, as Demeter's pale
   lamps give off light,
lead me then, lead the way.

Reach me a gentian, give me a torch!
let me guide myself with the blue, forked torch of this
   flower
down the darker and darker stairs, where blue is
   darkened on blueness
even where Persephone goes, just now, from the frosted
   September
to the sightless realm where darkness is awake upon
   the dark
and Persephone herself is but a voice
or a darkness invisible enfolded in the deeper dark

of the arms Plutonic, and pierced with the passion of dense
  gloom,
among the splendour of torches of darkness, shedding
  darkness on the lost bride and her groom.

D. H. LAWRENCE

Beech

They will not go. These leaves insist on staying.
Coinage like theirs looked frail six weeks ago.
What hintings at, excitement of delaying,
Almost as if some richer fruits could grow

If leaves hung on against each swipe of storm,
If branches bent but still did not give way.
Today is brushed with sun. The leaves are warm.
I picked one from the pavement and it lay

With borrowed shining on my Winter hand.
Persistence of this nature sends the pulse
Beating more rapidly. When will it end,

That pride of leaves? When will the branches be
Utterly bare, and seem like something else,
Now half-forgotten, no part of a tree?

ELIZABETH JENNINGS

Blackberries

for Jo

On the high iron railroad they drag their barbed wires
Through ditches, and twist
Up paths that look down over Consett, its fires gone out.
You are too young to remember.

But the sky is the colour of cold iron.
There is slag underfoot.
The hawthorn grows rusty. The dock rattles its seeds
Down the steep track. Each September,

Every year of our lives, Jo, we've climbed up here with
    buckets
Where the fat berries blacken on clinker.
The urge to pick them comes stronger than hunger.
Very soon, it says, it will be winter.

So fill your pails now for the time when there will be no
    blackberries.
Go home. Bottle them up,
Black as the midnight sky above the ironworks
Flaring red before the furnace doors clashed shut;

And over the sweet steam of the jam-pan, dream of
    December
And blackberries in February, and the shoots that already
Shove through the dust a gift from the dead to the living,
Older than words, Jo. As old as loving.

KATRINA PORTEOUS

Digging

Today I think
Only with scents, – scents dead leaves yield,
And bracken, and wild carrot's seed,
And the square mustard field;

Odours that rise
When the spade wounds the root of tree,
Rose, currant, raspberry, or goutweed,
Rhubarb or celery;

The smoke's smell, too
Flowing from where a bonfire burns
The dead, the waste, the dangerous,
And all to sweetness turns.

It is enough
To smell, to crumble the dark earth,
While the robin sings over again
Sad songs of Autumn mirth.

EDWARD THOMAS

'Fall, leaves, fall'

Fall, leaves, fall; die, flowers, away;
Lengthen night and shorten day;
Every leaf speaks bliss to me,
Fluttering from the autumn tree.

I shall smile when wreaths of snow
Blossom where the rose should grow;
I shall sing when night's decay
Ushers in a drearier day.

EMILY BRONTË

Gathering Mushrooms

The rain comes flapping through the yard
like a tablecloth that she hand-embroidered.
My mother has left it on the line.
It is sodden with rain.
The mushroom shed is windowless, wide,
its high-stacked wooden trays
hosed down with formaldehyde.
And my father has opened the Gates of Troy
to that first load of horse manure.
Barley straw. Gypsum. Dried blood. Ammonia.
Wagon after wagon
blusters in, a self-renewing gold-black dragon
we push to the back of the mind.
We have taken our pitchforks to the wind.

All brought back to me that September evening
fifteen years on. The pair of us
tripping through Barnett's fair demesne
like girls in long dresses
after a hail-storm.
We might have been thinking of the fire-bomb
that sent Malone House sky-high
and its priceless collection of linen
sky-high.
We might have wept with Elizabeth McCrum.
We were thinking only of psilocybin.
You sang of the maid you met on the dewy grass –
And she stooped so low gave me to know
it was mushrooms she was gathering O.

He'll be wearing that same old donkey-jacket
and the sawn-off waders.
He carries a knife, two punnets, a bucket.
He reaches far into his own shadow.
We'll have taken him unawares
and stand behind him, slightly to one side.
He is one of those ancient warriors
before the rising tide.
He'll glance back from under his peaked cap
without breaking rhythm:
his coaxing a mushroom – a flat or a cup –
the nick against his right thumb;
the bucket then, the punnet to left or right,
and so on and so forth till kingdom come.

We followed the overgrown towpath by the Lagan.
The sunset would deepen through cinnamon
to aubergine,
the wood-pigeon's concerto for oboe and strings,
allegro, blowing your mind.
And you were suddenly out of my ken, hurtling
towards the ever-receding ground,
into the maw
of a shimmering green-gold dragon.
You discovered yourself in some outbuilding
with your long-lost companion, me,
though my head had grown into the head of a horse
that shook its dirty-fair mane
and spoke this verse:

Come back to us. However cold and raw, your feet
were always meant
to negotiate terms with bare cement.

Beyond this concrete wall is a wall of concrete
and barbed wire. Your only hope
is to come back. If sing you must, let your song
tell of treading your own dung,
let straw and dung give a spring to your step.
If we never live to see the day we leap
into our true domain,
lie down with us now and wrap
yourself in the soiled grey blanket of Irish rain
that will, one day, bleach itself white.
Lie down with us and wait.

PAUL MULDOON

Hurrahing in Harvest

Summer ends now; now, barbarous in beauty, the stooks
   rise
Around; up above, what wind-walks! what lovely
   behaviour
Of silk-sack clouds! has wilder, wilful-wavier
Meal-drift moulded ever and melted across skies?

I walk, I lift up, I lift up heart, eyes,
Down all that glory in the heavens to glean our Saviour;
And, éyes, heárt, what looks, what lips yet gave you a
Rapturous love's greeting of realer, of rounder replies?

And the azurous hung hills are his world-wielding
   shoulder
Majestic – as a stallion stalwart, very-violet-sweet! –
These things, these things were here and but the beholder
Wanting; which two when they once meet,
The heart rears wings bold and bolder
And hurls for him, O half hurls earth for him off under
   his feet.

GERARD MANLEY HOPKINS

In the Rhine Valley

Die Farben der Bäume sind schön
And the sky's and the river's blue-greys
And the *Burg*, almost lost in the haze.

You're patient. You help me to learn
And you smile as I practise the phrase,
'Die Farben der Bäume sind schön.'

October. The year's on the turn –
It will take us our separate ways
But the sun shines. And we have two days.
Die Farben der Bäume sind schön.

WENDY COPE

Die Farben der Bäume sind schön] the colours of the trees are
beautiful   *Burg*] castle

In the Woods

Always at this time there is the bankrupt plant:
autumn afflicts the failed machinery of ferns with rust.
The foliage is full of broken windows.
The birch trees shed their aluminium crust,

and the cedar drops its complicated cogs.
The roof of things has fallen in –
these paprika patches on the factory floor
are corrugated remnants of protective tin.

Oddments blacken strangely on a nearby fence:
rags, an old glove in a liquorice droop,
washleathers warp with dull black holly claws.
It is a sad, abandoned, oddly human group.

The glove is singular. You cannot try it on.
It is too small. Besides, it has no fingers.
It is more like something surgical –
the unpleasant shape of stumpy enigmas.

Below, a nylon sock curls up like a dead animal.
Through a hole in the toe, a glint of teeth.
Over there, the remains of a fire –
pigeon feathers in a narrow ashy wreath.

And everywhere egg-shells, egg-shells,
so light they stir with the gentlest breath –
a breakfast of papery skulls. The Omelette Man
has eaten here and manufactured death.

CRAIG RAINE

[132]

November

No sun – no moon!
No morn – no noon –
No dawn –
No sky – no earthly view –
No distance looking blue –
No road – no street – no 't'other side the way' –
No end to any Row –
No indications where the Crescents go –
No top to any steeple –
No recognitions of familiar people –
No courtesies for showing 'em –
No knowing 'em!
No traveling at all – no locomotion,
No inkling of the way – no notion –
'No go' – by land or ocean –
No mail – no post –
No news from any foreign coast –
No park – no ring – no afternoon gentility –
No company – no nobility –
No warmth, no cheerfulness, no healthful ease,
  No comfortable feel in any member –
No shade, no shine, no butterflies, no bees,
No fruits, no flowers, no leaves, no birds,
  November!

THOMAS HOOD

November Songs

I

The air is rising tonight and the leaf dust is
   burning in cadmium bars, the skinny beeches
are alight in the town fire of their own humus.
   There is oxblood in the sky. No month to be surly.

The attic cracks and clicks as we ride the night
   our bodies spiced with salt and olive sweetness:
but a savoury smoke is hanging in our hair,
   for the earth turns, and the air of the earth rises.

And it blows November spores over the sash.
   The sky is a red lichen in the mirror,
as the air rises we already breathe in the
   oracular resins of the season.

II

And now what aureole possesses the fine
   extremities of my leafless trees? They are
Florentine today, their fen wood is ochre

an afternoon's bewildering last
   sunlight honours their sunken
life with an alien radiance:

and we, who are restless by the
   same accident that gives their
vegetable patience   grace

may worship the tranquillity of
   waiting, but will not
find such blessing in the human face.

                    ELAINE FEINSTEIN

Now is the Time for the Burning of the Leaves

Now is the time for the burning of the leaves.
They go to the fire; the nostril pricks with smoke
Wandering slowly into a weeping mist.
Brittle and blotched, ragged and rotten sheaves!
A flame seizes the smouldering ruin and bites
On stubborn stalks that crackle as they resist.

The last hollyhock's fallen tower is dust;
All the spices of June are a bitter reek,
All the extravagant riches spent and mean.
All burns! The reddest rose is a ghost;
Sparks whirl up, to expire in the mist: the wild
Fingers of fire are making corruption clean.

Now is the time for stripping the spirit bare,
Time for the burning of days ended and done,
Idle solace of things that have gone before:
Rootless hope and fruitless desire are there;
Let them go to the fire, with never a look behind.
The world that was ours is a world that is ours no more.

They will come again, the leaf and the flower, to arise
From squalor of rottenness into the old splendour,
And magical scents to a wondering memory bring;
The same glory, to shine upon different eyes.
Earth cares for her own ruins, naught for ours.
Nothing is certain, only the certain spring.

LAURENCE BINYON

October

Skies, big skies, careening over in the wind;
great shoals of cloud pitching and jostling
in their rush to be anywhere other than here.

You hesitate on your doorstep, glance up
and something tugs in your chest, rips free like a leaf
and is sucked up and away. Everything's

finished here: raw-boned sycamores,
fields scalped and sodden. The houses are shut
and dustbins roll in their own filth in the street.

So you would take your chances, risk it all . . .
You stand for a moment with the keys in your hand
feeling the pull of the sky and the moment passing.

JEAN SPRACKLAND

Oxfordshire

from The Scholar Gipsy

And, above Godstow Bridge, when hay-time's here
In June, and many a scythe in sunshine flames,
Men who through those wide fields of breezy grass
Where black-wing'd swallows haunt the glittering Thames,
To bathe in the abandon'd lasher pass,
Have often pass'd thee near
Sitting upon the river bank o'ergrown:
Mark'd thy outlandish garb, thy figure spare,
Thy dark vague eyes, and soft abstracted air;
But, when they came from bathing, thou wert gone.

At some lone homested in the Cumnor hills,
Where at her open door the housewife darns,
Thou has been seen, or hanging on a gate
To watch the threshers in the mossy barns.
Children, who early range these slopes and late
For cresses from the rills,
Have known thee watching, all an April day,
The springing pastures and the feeding kine;
And mark'd thee, when the stars come out and shine,
Through the long dewy grass move slow away.

In Autumn, on the skirts of Bagley wood,
Where most the Gipsies by the turf-edg'd way
Pitch their smok'd tents, and every bush you see
With scarlet patches tagg'd and shreds of grey,
Above the forest ground call'd Thessaly –
The blackbird picking food

Sees thee, nor stops his meal, nor fears at all;
So often has he known thee past him stray
Rapt, twirling in thy hand a wither'd spray,
And waiting for the spark from Heaven to fall.

MATTHEW ARNOLD

Poem in October

It was my thirtieth year to heaven
Woke to my hearing from harbour and neighbour wood
And the mussel pooled and the heron
Priested shore
The morning beckon
With water praying and call of seagull and rook
And the knock of sailing boats on the net webbed wall
Myself to set foot
That second
In the still sleeping town and set forth.

My birthday began with the water –
Birds and the birds of the winged trees flying my name
Above the farms and the white horses
And I rose
In rainy autumn
And walked abroad in a shower of all my days.
High tide and the heron dived when I took the road
Over the border
And the gates
Of the town closed as the town awoke.

A springful of larks in a rolling
Cloud and the roadside bushes brimming with whistling
Blackbirds and the sun of October
Summery
On the hill's shoulder,
Here were fond climates and sweet singers suddenly
Come in the morning where I wandered and listened
To the rain wringing

Wind blow cold
In the wood faraway under me.

Pale rain over the dwindling harbour
And over the sea wet church the size of a snail
With its horns through mist and the castle
Brown as owls
But all the gardens
Of spring and summer were blooming in the tall tales
Beyond the border and under the lark full cloud.
There could I marvel
My birthday
Away but the weather turned around.

It turned away from the blithe country
And down the other air and the blue altered sky
Streamed again a wonder of summer
With apples
Pears and red currants
And I saw in the turning so clearly a child's
Forgotten mornings when he walked with his mother
Through the parables
Of sun light
And the legends of the green chapels

And the twice told fields of infancy
That his tears burned my cheeks and his heart moved in mine.
These were the woods the river and sea
Where a boy
In the listening
Summertime of the dead whispered the truth of his joy
To the trees and the stones and the fish in the tide.
And the mystery

Sang alive
Still in the water and singingbirds.

And there could I marvel my birthday
Away but the weather turned around. And the true
Joy of the long dead child sang burning
In the sun.
It was my thirtieth
Year to heaven stood there then in the summer noon
Though the town below lay leaved with October blood.
O may my heart's truth
Still be sung
On this high hill in a year's turning.

DYLAN THOMAS

Poppies in October

Even the sun-clouds this morning cannot manage such
  skirts.
Nor the woman in the ambulance
Whose red heart blooms through her coat so
  astoundingly –

A gift, a love gift
Utterly unasked for
By a sky

Palely and flamily
Igniting its carbon monoxides, by eyes
Dulled to a halt under bowlers.

O my God, what am I
That these late mouths should cry open
In a forest of frost, in a dawn of cornflowers.

SYLVIA PLATH

Postscript

And some time make the time to drive out west
Into County Clare, along the Flaggy Shore,
In September or October, when the wind
And the light are working off each other
So that the ocean on one side is wild
With foam and glitter, and inland among stones
The surface of a slate-grey lake is lit
By the earthed lightning of a flock of swans,
Their feathers roughed and ruffling, white on white,
Their fully grown headstrong-looking heads
Tucked or cresting or busy underwater.
Useless to think you'll park or capture it
More thoroughly. You are neither here nor there,
A hurry through which known and strange things pass
As big soft buffetings come at the car sideways
And catch the heart off guard and blow it open.

SEAMUS HEANEY

To Autumn

Season of mists and mellow fruitfulness,
  Close bosom-friend of the maturing sun;
Conspiring with him how to load and bless
  With fruit the vines that round the thatch-eves run;
To bend with apples the moss'd cottage-trees,
  And fill all fruit with ripeness to the core;
    To swell the gourd, and plump the hazel shells
With a sweet kernel; to set budding more,
  And still more, later flowers for the bees,
    Until they think warm days will never cease,
For Summer has o'er-brimm'd their clammy cells.

Who hath not seen thee oft amid thy store?
  Sometimes whoever seeks abroad may find
Thee sitting careless on a granary floor,
  Thy hair soft-lifted by the winnowing wind;
Or on a half-reap'd furrow sound asleep,
  Drows'd with the fume of poppies, while thy hook
    Spares the next swath and all its twined flowers:
And sometimes like a gleaner thou dost keep
  Steady thy laden head across a brook;
  Or by a cyder-press, with patient look,
    Thou watchest the last oozings hours by hours.

Where are the songs of Spring? Ay, where are they?
  Think not of them, thou hast thy music too, –
While barred clouds bloom the soft-dying day,
  And touch the stubble-plains with rosy hue;

Then in a wailful choir the small gnats mourn
　　Among the river sallows, borne aloft
　　　Or sinking as the light wind lives or dies;
And full-grown lambs loud bleat from hilly bourn;
　　Hedge-crickets sing; and now with treble soft
　　The red-breast whistles from a garden-croft;
　　　And gathering swallows twitter in the skies.

JOHN KEATS

The Wild Swans at Coole

The trees are in their autumn beauty,
The woodland paths are dry,
Under the October twilight the water
Mirrors a still sky;
Upon the brimming water among the stones
Are nine-and-fifty swans.

The nineteenth autumn has come upon me
Since I first made my count;
I saw, before I had well finished,
All suddenly mount
And scatter wheeling in great broken rings
Upon their clamorous wings.

I have looked upon those brilliant creatures,
And now my heart is sore.
All's changed since I, hearing at twilight,
The first time on this shore,
The bell-beat of their wings above my head,
Trod with a lighter tread.

Unwearied still, lover by lover,
They paddle in the cold
Companionable streams or climb the air;
Their hearts have not grown old;
Passion or conquest, wander where they will,
Attend upon them still.

But now they drift on the still water,
Mysterious, beautiful;
Among what rushes will they build,
By what lake's edge or pool
Delight men's eyes when I awake some day
To find they have flown away?

W. B. YEATS

NOW I have told the year from dawn to dusk

Now I have told the year from dawn to dusk,
its morning and its evening and its noon
Once round the sun our slanting orbit rolls

'Now I have told the year from dawn to dusk'

Now I have told the year from dawn to dusk,
Its morning and its evening and its noon;
Once round the sun our slanting orbit rolled,
Four times the seasons changed, thirteen the moon;
Corn grew from seed to husk,
The young spring grass to provender for herds;
Drought came, and earth was grateful for the rain;
The bees streamed in and out the summer hives;
Birds wildly sang; were silent; birds
With summer's passing fitfully sang again;
The loaded waggon crossed the field; the sea
Spread her great generous pasture as a robe
Whereon the slow ships, circling statelily,
Are patterned round the globe.
The ample busyness of life went by,
All the full busyness of lives
Unknown to fame, made lovely by no words:
The shepherd lonely in the winter fold;
The tiller following the eternal plough
Beneath a stormy or a gentle sky;
The sower with his gesture like a gift
Walking the furrowed hill from base to brow;
The reaper in the piety of thrift
Binding the sheaf against his slanted thigh.

VITA SACKVILLE-WEST

On Change of Weathers

And were it for thy profit, to obtaine
All *Sunshine*? No vicissitude of *Raine*?
Thinkst thou, that thy laborious *Plough* requires
Not Winter *frosts*, as well as Summer *fiers*?
There must be both: Sometimes these hearts of ours
Must have the sweet, the seasonable Showers
Of *Teares*; Sometimes the Frost of chill *despaire*
Makes our desired *sunshine* seeme more *faire*:
Weathers that most oppose the Flesh and Blood,
Are such as helpe to make our *Harvest* good:
We may not choose, great *God*: It is thy *Task*:
We know not what to *have*; nor how to ask.

FRANCIS QUARLES

Weathers

This is the weather the cuckoo likes,
    And so do I;
When showers betumble the chestnut spikes,
    And nestlings fly:
And the little brown nightingale bills his best,
And they sit outside at 'The Travellers' Rest,'
And maids come forth sprig-muslin drest,
And citizens dream of the south and west,
    And so do I.

This is the weather the shepherd shuns,
    And so do I;
When beeches drip in browns and duns,
    And thresh, and ply;
And hill-hid tides throb, throe on throe,
And meadow rivulets overflow,
And drops on gate-bars hang in a row,
And rooks in families homeward go,
    And so do I.

THOMAS HARDY

Acknowledgements

∾

SIMON ARMITAGE: 'Dew' from *Stanza Stones* (Enitharmon, 2013) © Simon Armitage and reproduced by permission of Enitharmon Press

W. H. AUDEN: 'Autumn Song' and 'Summer Night' from *Collected Poems*, ed. Edward Mendelson (Faber & Faber, 1976) reproduced by permission of Curtis Brown Ltd

LAURENCE BINYON: 'Now is the time for the burning of the leaves' reproduced by permission of the Society of Authors as the Literary Representative of the Estate of Laurence Binyon

GILLIAN CLARKE: 'Neighbours' from *Collected Poems* (Carcanet, 1997) © the author and reproduced by permission of Carcanet Press Ltd

WENDY COPE: 'In the Rhine Valley' and 'The Christmas Life' from *Serious Concerns* (Faber & Faber, 1992) © Wendy Cope and reproduced by permission of Faber & Faber Ltd and Farrar, Straus and Giroux Ltd

ELAINE FEINSTEIN: 'November Songs' from *Collected Poems & Translations* (Carcanet, 2002) © the author and reproduced by permission of Carcanet Press Ltd

LAVINIA GREENLAW: 'Heliotropical' from *Minsk* (Faber & Faber, 2003) © Lavinia Greenlaw and reproduced by permission of Faber & Faber Ltd

IAN HAMILTON: 'Midwinter' from *Collected Poems* (Faber & Faber, 2009) © The Estate of Ian Hamilton and reproduced by permission of Faber & Faber Ltd

SEAMUS HEANEY: 'Death of a Naturalist' from *Death of a Naturalist*; 'The Trees of Ireland' from *Sweeney Astray* and 'Postscript' from *The Spirit Level* (Faber & Faber, 1966, 1983, 1986) © The Estate of Seamus Heaney and reproduced by permission of Faber & Faber Ltd and Farrar, Straus and Giroux LLC in the United States